So Much Better Bible Study

TYNDALE
MOMENTUM™

A Tyndale nonfiction imprint

Kaci Nicole Harlow

so much better

BIBLE STUDY

a six-week journey to trusting God while you wait

Visit Tyndale online at tyndale.com.

Visit the author online at kacinicole.com.

Visit Tyndale Christian Resources at tyndalechristianresources.com.

So Much Better Bible Study: A Six-Week Journey to Trusting God While You Wait

Cover design by Libby Dykstra

Interior design by Brandi Davis

Edited by Stephanie Rische

Published in association with Teresa Evenson Author Media Services, T.E.A.M. Services.

ISBN 979-8-4005-0317-7

Printed in China

32 31 30 29 28 27 26
7 6 5 4 3 2 1

contents

	Introduction	1
	How to Use This Study	3
	A Note to the Leader	7
SESSION 1	Healing in the Waiting	11
SESSION 2	Intimacy in the Waiting	29
SESSION 3	Faith in the Waiting	45
SESSION 4	Humility in the Waiting	61
SESSION 5	Fruitfulness in the Waiting	77
SESSION 6	Transformation in the Waiting	95
	Small Group Lesson Plans	113
	About the Author	125

introduction

What is that thing for you? That thing you've been praying for and waiting on for months, years, maybe even decades? What is the circumstance that hasn't seemed to change, that makes you struggle to see how God is good to you or working in your life at all?

I don't know what that thing is for you, but I do know that each of us has (at least) one: Maybe it's marriage or motherhood, healing from a health condition or buying a home, getting out of debt or discovering God's purpose for your life. Maybe you're waiting for a prodigal child to return or a deployment to end, or maybe you want to know what's going to happen in an area of seemingly unending uncertainty.

When we're waiting on God and He seems silent, it can bring up a whole slew of questions. *I know God is good to others, but is He good to me? What am I supposed to do with these desires? Does God want me to let go of them or continue waiting? What is the purpose of this season God has me in? Why does it seem like God is closing door after door after door?*

Dear reader, I know the anguish of these heart questions, because I've asked them myself. I've wrestled through them. I asked and wrestled as I walked through most of my twenties being single, watching my best friends become brides and welcome baby after baby—all the while longing to be a wife and mama myself. And although the things I'm waiting on now may be a little less raw, I've come to learn that all of life involves waiting of some kind. I can choose to stay focused on the thing I'm waiting for: certainty with career developments, having my baby sleep through the night, updating our home. Or I can shift my focus: What is God teaching me *through* this wait? And that's exactly what I've found in my seasons of waiting: It's often through the very circumstances we're wishing God would change that He's wanting to change *us*.

This isn't to say God doesn't care about our desires, because He does. And His purposes for each of our lives are oh-so-good. But God also cares deeply about who we are *becoming* while we wait. God often uses the things we long for in this life as a sort of leverage in the process of sanctification to draw us deeper into His heart and make us look more like Him.

The choice we face is how we will navigate our waiting. Will we become bitter and resentful in the waiting, perhaps hardening ourselves to God? Or will we accept this waiting season as an invitation to dig deeper into His heart and His Word?

how to use this study

God's Word is how we know God and grow to look more like Him. Maybe the Bible is familiar to you, or maybe this is kind of a new idea. Either way, think about how incredible this truth is: The God of the universe has given us a way to get to know Him! And He delights in revealing Himself to us so we don't have to stay stuck where we are.

I have a deep love for studying God's Word. I got a degree studying the Bible in college, and by God's grace, it's the heart of what I do for work too—on the fringe hours of my full-time and favorite job, which is being a mama. I have an online ministry where I share biblical truth and encouragement through YouTube videos and Instagram content. (Check out kacinicole.com if you want to find out more.)

My prayer is that Scripture will shape how I show up each day as a wife, a mama to littles, a friend, a daughter, and a small group leader. The reason I wrote this Bible study is because I believe God does transformational work in our lives through His Word. This study you're holding in your hands now is a companion to my book, *So Much Better*, in which I detail how God used my decade-long desire to be married to reveal things in my heart that were misaligned and to refine me more into His image. It includes my personal stories, hard-fought lessons, biblical truths, and the gold nuggets I gleaned along the way.

I encourage you to read *So Much Better* alongside this study as we journey together in getting to know God's heart more deeply and gaining confidence that He is working in significant ways, even in our waiting. I recommend either reading the main book first and following up with this study or working through the book and Bible study in tandem. I've included a note at the beginning of each session about which chapters of the book to read alongside that week's homework if you choose to go through both books together.

As you read the book, think of this study as a friend who will help you unpack the biblical truth and encouragement from each chapter and apply it to your own life. In other words, this is where we'll put it into practice—asking God what He wants us to do with what we've read and how He might be inviting us to change the way we think and live.

In this study, we'll unpack six of the specific ways God tends to work in our waiting: bringing healing to our hearts and lives, deepening our intimacy with Him, building our faith, humbling us, producing fruit in us, and transforming us more into His image. We'll dive deeper into some of the key biblical passages I touch on in *So Much Better*, allowing space for personal reflection and application.

Each session includes a supplemental video teaching that can be watched either individually or with a group at the start of the week. (You'll see that I've included a blank page at the beginning of each session where you can take notes from the video.) Next, there is individual homework to help you process the material throughout the week. Each week's homework includes the profile of a woman in waiting, a brief devotional, reflection questions, a prayer, and a Scripture passage to memorize. This section is intended to be flexible to fit your unique schedule or life stage. You can choose to do a little bit of the homework every day and tie it in with your personal devotional time, or you can dedicate one day a week to the homework and do it all in one sitting. Finally, small group lesson plans are included in the final section of this study if you choose to go through it with other people. Feel free to use what's helpful—if the first question leads to good heart conversations, don't feel like you need to cut the conversation short so you can get through all the questions. Let the Holy Spirit lead.

My prayer is that as we dive deeply into the Word of God, you would grow to love the God of the Word more deeply, you would come to see that His heart for you is good, and your eyes would be opened to see just how present and active He is in your life right now, even in the middle of the waiting—whether you're waiting for something big or small. And I pray that your life would look and feel different—for the better—as a result.

Every trial along our journey is simply a tool in the hand of God, who cares about our sanctification. Not only so we can become brides or mothers or so we can thrive in the callings He has given us, but because we are the bride of Christ—and He is committed to making us blameless before Him on that day when we see Him face-to-face (see Ephesians 5:27).

What if God's goodness isn't only available to you on the other side of the waiting but right here in the middle of it? What if there's something significant He wants to do in you right here and now—perhaps even more significant than whatever it is you're waiting for?

As I've learned in my own journey of waiting, as well as on the pages of Scripture, that's exactly His intent. He has good plans that aren't just something we can live with or something we can make work. He has in mind something that's better than we could imagine—so much better.

Much love,

Kaci

a note to the leader

God has specifically chosen *you* to lead this particular group of women in this exact season of life. He has a plan and a purpose for the things you'll learn together, the prayers you'll lift up together, and the life you'll walk through together over these next six weeks. He knows everything that will unfold and how He will work through it. God has called you to lead this group, and He has given you everything you need to see it through. "His divine power has given us everything we need for a godly life through our knowledge of him who called us by his own glory and goodness" (2 Peter 1:3, NIV). How encouraging is that?

I know how nerve-racking and vulnerable it can feel to lead a small group. You worry: *Will it be awkward? Will people connect? Will they feel like they're getting something valuable out of this? Will they like me? Will they want to come back?*

Here's the good news, though: The results don't rest on you. The only measure of success is your obedience to God and your faithfulness in showing up each week. God is in control of the rest. The truth is, you might feel a little awkward at first. You might second-guess whether people will be glad they came. You might feel like you try to start conversations and they struggle to take off. But keep at it. In time, God will use your faithfulness to build something beautiful.

A few practical tips before you begin . . .

- Share a snack or a meal together each week. It doesn't have to be fancy or homemade—it can be store-bought and enjoyed on paper plates. You also don't need to be the one in charge of food each week. I've found that inviting others to participate in this way gives everyone a sense of ownership in the group, and it relieves some of the pressure on you as the leader. Even if it's simple, there's something about sharing food together that breaks down walls and invites more intimate fellowship. One of my favorite ways to transition from eating to the study portion is to have everyone share a high and low from the week. Sometimes people share things that are lighthearted, and it simply breaks the ice. Other times, you'll be surprised at the raw vulnerability this simple question invites. Either way, doing this gives insight into what each person is going through and offers each person an opportunity to be known and supported in those areas.
- Pray, pray, pray. On your own, pray that God would move powerfully through the group and reveal Himself to each person. Pray, as you begin your time together, that God would work in and through the conversations and that they would help each person to know Him more. And pray as you end your time together, inviting people to share their requests and recognizing that there is power in bearing one another's burdens and lifting them up to God.
- Last but certainly not least, remember (and ask God to help you remember) that there's no need to prove yourself. Take a moment and read that again. You don't have to be a Bible scholar, you don't need a ton of experience leading small groups, and you don't need the perfect home or really anything else to lead this study aside from what God has already given you fully: *Himself.* Simply offer who you are and what you have, and do your best to share honestly and ask good questions to cultivate conversation. But remember that God's Spirit dwells in you and that *He* is the one who will do the important heart work.

I'm praying for you as you go through this study, that it would point you powerfully to the character of God, that it would help you know Him more, that you would draw deeper in community with those in your group, that you would be encouraged with rich biblical truths, and that you would know God is working in whatever you're walking through.

I'm cheering you on and praying you through! Now let's dig in.

VIDEO SESSION 1 NOTES

healing in the waiting

To access the video session, use the instructions in the front of your Bible study book.

journal entry of a modern-day bleeding woman

Healing in the Waiting

Inspired by Mark 5:25-34

Another set of labs came back today: inconclusive. Why did I think it would be any different this time? It's always the same story: No clear answers, only another hypothesis to test, another food to cut from my diet, another supplement to add to my already overflowing weekly pillbox. And after I do all of that, yet again, I wait—to see if any of my efforts made a difference. But they probably won't. Not for long, anyway—that's how it always goes. Meanwhile, I continue to live day in and day out with this constant discomfort and pain. Lord, I'm Just. So. Tired.

Don't You hear my pleas? I'm asking for Your wisdom like You tell me to in Your Word. I'm begging You to direct me to a doctor who can uncover the root cause. I'm desperate for You to show me what lifestyle changes I need to make. I'll do anything. Lord, I'm asking You to do what only You can do: to free me from this ailment I've lived with for as long as I can remember. I long to touch the hem of Your garment, to be made instantly whole. I have faith. I know with everything in me that You can do it. But You're not. Why? How long must I endure?

Yet this I call to mind, and so I have hope: Your mercies are new every morning. I've lived this truth, even in the middle of my longing. Every day, You sustain me. When I wake and the pain screams at me and I wonder how I'll make it through another day, You carry me. Though I'm still waiting for physical healing, I sense You doing a deeper healing in my heart. You're uncovering things, like my bent toward self-sufficiency. Many days, I have no choice but to ask for help. You're teaching me how to let others in and how to humbly receive. You're teaching me how to rewrite the track of constant anxiety that plays in my mind. Instead of always fearing the worst, I'm learning that even in *the worst, You are there with me. And with every whisper spoken over me in Your Word, with every tangible sense of comfort I've felt as I've cried out to You, You're showing me what it's like to be cared for by You as my loving Father. You're untangling lies with deep roots—that I have to handle it all on my own, that I have to be prepared for anything that could go wrong, and that it all depends on me. I know now it doesn't.*

Lord, I'm seeking You. I'm pressing through the crowds of fear and lies that fight to cloud my mind to draw near to You, to get even a glimpse. I hope and I pray and I long for the day when You will turn, our eyes will meet, and You'll tell me, "Daughter, your faith has made you well." Oh, what a day that will be. But even as I wait for You to do an external work in my physical body, I thank You, Lord, for all the important work You are doing inside me.

SESSION 1

healing in the waiting

To get the most out of this week's study, read chapters 1–4 of So Much Better.

Imagine you're on a hike when you notice there's a pebble in your shoe. It starts to irritate your heel, so you wiggle your foot around a bit, hoping that will solve the problem. You don't want to have to stop and interrupt your hike. But the more you press on, the more the pebble presses into *you*—and it starts to hurt. Finally, you have no choice. The pain is so intense that you're forced to sit down, take off your shoe, and remove the pebble. But when you do, you find something much more serious than a pebble. You see that, completely unrelated to the pebble, your foot is suffering from some sort of injury or infection. Suddenly, you're grateful for that annoying little pebble. No longer is it merely a nuisance that was slowing you down. You see that it alerted you to something much more urgent that needed to be addressed.

It's sort of a gross analogy, I'll admit. But I think this is a fitting picture of how God often works in our lives. We might wonder why He allows us to walk through the heartbreak or the job loss or the season of struggle that seems like it will never end. We view the waiting as a nuisance, and we wish we could wiggle it away so we could continue on our way and get on to the good stuff. But oh, the goodness of our God. Yes, He cares about our journey. Yes, He will see us through to the end. But what we're waiting for isn't the only "good stuff." God cares about our desires, but He also cares about the deeper things that need to be healed in the here and now, and He sometimes uses the waiting to address them.

1. What currently feels like a pebble in your life—a nagging circumstance you wish God would remove?

2. Have you sat down to address the pebble and bring it before God? Or are you trying to push through and ignore it?

3. What area of your life that's in need of healing might God be revealing through the waiting? If you aren't sure, ask Him to show you!

Sometimes what needs healing is a hard thing that happened to us in our past that we may be unaware of—or maybe we *are* aware, but we've tried to press it down. Other times what's in need of healing is hurt or shame from our own sin or past mistakes. Regardless of the cause, God longs for our healing. It's easy to see our deep need for healing and feel a frantic pressure to be fully healed. But freedom doesn't rest on us. God asks for our participation, but He is our ultimate healer. The work He does in our lives takes time, but He won't stop until it's complete.

The mere fact that God has revealed an area of our hearts in need of healing is itself evidence that He is already at work and will see it through. Inevitably, this process involves God inviting us to step into the light. It can be scary to bring the parts of ourselves in need of healing before Him and others. But as we talk about in chapter 4 of *So Much Better*, healing doesn't come from hiding.

4. Read this verse slowly. What does God say is necessary in order to experience healing?

> Confess your sins to one another and pray for one another, that you may be healed.
>
> **JAMES 5:16**

God cares about our desires, but He also cares about the deeper things that need to be healed in the here and now.

5. **Now read this verse slowly. What does God say is necessary to experience forgiveness and cleansing?**

> If we confess our sins, he is faithful and just to forgive us our sins and to cleanse us from all unrighteousness.
> **1 JOHN 1:9**

God brings things into the light not to expose us or shame us, but to heal and free us. Like I talk about in chapter 4, when I share the story of my childhood home being renovated, mold grows in the dark. The same is true of sin and shame. The more we try to hide those things from God, others, or even ourselves, the more they grow and compound. We can't simply pretend that sin or shame isn't there and hope it will go away on its own; we have to bring it into the light. We have to allow it to be exposed.

Being exposed is scary. Terrifying, even. It makes you feel naked and vulnerable. The enemy will whisper, *What will people think?* in an attempt to keep you hidden. But in the appropriate context, confession doesn't lead to shame—it actually *frees* us from shame. When we hide certain parts of our hearts or lives, we live in continual fear of being exposed, found out. But when we bring the hard things out of the dark and into the light, we can live in freedom, knowing we aren't defined by those things—we're defined by the blood of Christ, which washes us clean.

God promises in 1 John 1:9 that when we confess our sins, He will forgive us and cleanse us from all unrighteousness. It doesn't say that if we confess our sins, He *might* forgive us, if the offense wasn't too bad or if He's in a good mood or if we're sorry enough. It says He *will*. We don't have to guess how He'll react. He tells us plain and clear. Through confession, we can come before God in confidence, knowing we will receive His forgiveness and cleansing because of Jesus alone. How comforting is that?

6. Is there any sin in your life you have been attempting to minimize (*I don't do it that often*), defend (*I only do it because so-and-so did this*), or hide (*I'm afraid other people would view me differently if they found out*)? Write it down. Confess it to God in your heart.

7. Are there any hurts in your life God might be prompting you to talk to Him or another person about? Write them down. Bring them before God in prayer.

Now I encourage you to spend some time praying about who God might be leading you to confide in about these things. There is power in bringing them into the light in the context of confession to another person—but doing so requires discernment to know *who* to share with. Be thoughtful and prayerful about this decision. God might lead you to share with your small group, or He might lead you to share with someone you have established trust with. Pray about it, and know that God will bring the right person to mind.

Tip: If someone is willing to consistently talk to you about the sins and shortcomings of another person, they probably aren't the best person to confess yours to. You'll want to look for someone who isn't out for gossip but will be there to encourage you, hold you accountable, and point you to the truth of God's Word. You'll want to confess to someone who will help guide you away from sin, not toward it.

8. Who might God be leading you to practice confession with?

One of the keys to confessing our sins to God is recognizing the character of the One we're confessing to. If we fear He's a cruel master who delights in punishing us, we won't feel safe to be honest with Him. If we think He's nice but powerless, there's no point in confessing to Him. But if we believe He is both merciful and powerful to forgive us and free us of our sin—if we accept the true gospel—we'll be able to come before Him with confidence and raw honesty.

9. In your own words, how would you explain the gospel?

Even though I grew up in a Christian home and went to a Christian school and church, for a long time I struggled to be able to put the gospel clearly and concisely into words. But knowing how to do so is crucial, because the gospel gives us a framework to understand everything we go through in this life—even and especially the hard things and the prayers we're waiting to be answered.

In chapter 3 of *So Much Better*, we talk about a four-part framework for understanding and articulating the gospel that has been incredibly helpful to me. Let's review it here:

Creation: God created the heavens and the earth and everything in them. He created people to exist in perfect relationship with Himself, and He called all He created good. The earth was full of peace and human flourishing; everything was as it should be.

Turn to Genesis 1:31 and write the Scripture here:

Fall: Sin entered God's world through Satan. Adam and Eve bought into his deception that God was withholding good from them, and they rejected God's rule—and we followed in their footsteps. We rebel against God and go our own way, becoming God's enemies. The effects of sin come in the form of pain, suffering, destruction, and death—physical, relational, and spiritual.

Turn to Romans 3:23 and write the Scripture here:

Redemption: God sent Jesus, His one and only perfect Son, to die on the cross for our sins. Then God raised Him to life again so that whoever believes in Him will not die but will have everlasting life. Jesus' death and resurrection provide a way for us to be redeemed; this is the cornerstone of the gospel.

Turn to John 3:16 and write the Scripture here:

Restoration: God is taking this broken, fallen world and restoring it, ushering in His Kingdom and glory and making things right again. One day Jesus will return and defeat Satan once and for all. The Kingdom of God in its fullness will restore the fallenness of humanity, and those who have put their faith in Jesus Christ as Lord and Savior will live with Him forever in perfect joy and peace.

Turn to Revelation 21:5 and write the Scripture here:

Understanding this framework—and particularly, where we are situated in it—is key. You and I are living between redemption and restoration, in what theologians sometimes call "the already but not yet." Jesus has already defeated death, but we have not yet seen sin and its effects fully eradicated from our hearts and the world we live in. Jesus has already gone to the cross, but He has not yet returned to establish His eternal reign. This means that for those of us who are in Christ, God has already begun to free us from fears, heal us of hurts, strip us of sin, and make us look more like Him. But we haven't yet experienced the completion of those things. We still wrestle with fear, wait for God to heal hurts, and need to be cleansed of our sin. Yet in Jesus, we have the assurance that we will one day experience the completion of His plan of restoration.

10. How does this gospel framework bring insight and perspective to the hard circumstance you wish God would remove from your life?

11. Look up Philippians 1:6 (ESV) and fill in the missing word. "I am sure of this, that he who began a good work in you will bring it to ______________________ at the day of Jesus Christ."

Completion = the state of being finished.

God won't stop His work in you until it's complete.

12. How does this truth bring perspective and comfort to the areas of waiting in your life?

13. Romans 5:3-5 says, "Not only that, but we rejoice in our sufferings, knowing that suffering produces endurance, and endurance produces character, and character produces hope, and hope does not put us to shame, because God's love has been poured into our hearts through the Holy Spirit who has been given to us." **How do you see God using your waiting to develop your character and make you look more like Him? Spend some time thanking God for the hope you have in Him!**

Prayer

God, I acknowledge that this circumstance feels like a pebble in my shoe. I wish You would just remove it, but I understand that You may want to show me something through it. Reveal any areas of my heart that are in need of healing. Reveal any sin or lie that I need to bring before You. Show me who I should practice confession with. Thank You that You make all things new and that You will not abandon the work of Your hands. I can rest knowing You will bring the work You're doing in my life to completion. Show me how You're developing my character through the waiting. Make me look more like You. In Jesus' name, amen.

Hide God's Word in Your Heart

Which key verse from this week's study stood out to you most? Highlight it and practice memorizing it this week.

> If we confess our sins, he is faithful and just to forgive us our sins and to cleanse us from all unrighteousness.
> **1 JOHN 1:9**

> I am sure of this, that he who began a good work in you will bring it to completion at the day of Jesus Christ.
> **PHILIPPIANS 1:6**

> We rejoice in our sufferings, knowing that suffering produces endurance, and endurance produces character, and character produces hope, and hope does not put us to shame, because God's love has been poured into our hearts through the Holy Spirit who has been given to us.
> **ROMANS 5:3-5**

Spend some time reflecting on what you learned in this study and what small step you can take toward applying it to your life this week.

VIDEO SESSION 2 NOTES

intimacy in the waiting

To access the video session, use the instructions in the front of your Bible study book.

journal entry of a modern-day Hannah

Intimacy in the Waiting

Inspired by 1 Samuel 1

Lord, so much of my life feels like it's everything I ever wanted. A husband I love, meaningful work to do, rich community surrounding us. Yet sometimes all I can see is the one thing that feels missing.

When we open our home to friends (who are more like family), I'm filled with gratitude to do life with people we can laugh with, cry with, pray with. But as I set the table once more and pull out tiny silicone forks that we only ever use for company, I feel a stabbing ache in my heart. The silverware stares up at me as if it were a jealous sister-wife, mocking me in my area of lack—even as I pour myself out in prayer at Your feet.

There are days, even weeks, when my life feels so full of good things that I'm able to shift my focus entirely. I don't think about it much at all. But like clockwork, every month I'm met with a cruel reminder I can't ignore. It washes me with new waves of grief and frustration—and sometimes even anger. It's a physical reminder that I'm still without. It's a testament to the truth that neither ancient wisdom nor modern medicine, while both good gifts, can open a womb. That's something only You can do.

Lord, I love to hear the laughter of our friends' kids fill our home. But I long to know: When will our kids get to join in? While I love to host baby showers and show up for kids' birthday parties, I can't ignore my own longing: When will we get to mark these occasions for our own children? I love being "Auntie," but the silent, pervasive question of my heart persists: When will I get to be Mom?

In the pain, I've come to know Your heart like never before. I always heard that You wipe away tears. But now I've experienced You wiping mine—through the strong but tender hands of my husband and through the friends who are willing to simply sit with me in the sadness, not feeling a need to say anything at all. In the pain, I've sensed Your presence more tangibly than ever before. You, Lord, are close to the brokenhearted, indeed.

You are the God who sees me when my heart feels sad. Your Spirit intercedes for me when I don't have the words to pray. You're with me when I feel utterly alone. Lord, I don't understand what You're doing, but I know that You're with me. And this unmet desire is the thorn in my flesh that keeps me dependent on You and pressing into You.

I bring before You my deep desire to have a child, to be a mother. Lord, do what only You can do! You, God, are the Giver of life and the Giver of every good gift. I know that all of it belongs to You—every blessing You've already poured out and the ones I hope You still will.

SESSION 2

intimacy in the waiting

To get the most out of this week's study, read chapters 5–7 of So Much Better.

My toddler recently started doing something that melts me. Whenever he gets hurt, he holds up whichever body part has been affected, looks at me, and says, "Kiss?" He's an increasingly independent boy who loves to climb, run, and do all the daring things—constantly keeping this mama on her toes. But whenever he's hurting, he knows exactly where to go: straight to his mama for a kiss and maybe a few cuddles that will make it "all better" before he's off to the races again.

This is how we often interact with God. When life is all roses, it's easy to be independent and forget our need for Him. We can go days, weeks, even months without truly connecting with Him. But the thorns of life, as painful as they may be, keep us pressing into Him. The thorns keep us crying out to God—for relief, for comfort, for answers. I don't believe God *causes* our pain like some cruel parent who trips His child so they will run to Him to make it all better. But I do believe He *allows* the pain we experience in this fallen world—and He refuses to waste it. He uses it to draw us deeper into His heart and to forge an intimacy with us that we often don't seek in the same way when everything is going well.

There's something about waiting in particular that offers us an invitation to intimacy with the Lord. Day after day, you're waiting for those finances to come through. Month after month, you're waiting for that positive pregnancy test. Year after year, you're waiting for the right person to finally walk into your life . . . and stay. With each day that passes without receiving the thing you're waiting for, the ache grows. It weighs heavy on your heart. You ask, *Why, God? Are You ever going to give me this thing? Why are You allowing this to happen? Please, Lord, see the desires of my heart.*

I assure you: God sees, hears, and knows. And you will see that He has a good plan for you—whenever and however it unfolds. But there's something unique about this time right now. It might not seem like it in the middle of the pain, but on the other side, you're likely to look back and see it as a season of precious closeness with the Lord—depending on how you approach it.

1. How has your season of waiting or pain affected your faith? Have you allowed this challenge to harden your heart, or is it keeping you desperately pressing into God?

If your pain is keeping you pressing into God, ask Him to show you how He is using it to build your relationship so He can encourage you while you wait. If you feel hardened to God in your pain, ask Him to soften your heart and gently reveal any lies you may believe about His character so He can reveal His tender love and care for you.

Now spend some time meditating on Ezekiel 34. Read the chapter once out loud, then simply listen to it a second time with your eyes closed. (YouVersion is a great free Bible app that will read any passage of Scripture out loud for you.)

2. What do you notice about God's posture toward His people (or, to use the language of the text, His "sheep") in this passage? Write down any observations about this or anything else that stands out to you.

3. Fill in all the promises of God from Ezekiel 34, designated when God says, "I will":

- God will __________ for His sheep and will seek them out. (Ezekiel 34:11)
- God will __________ His sheep from all places where they have been scattered. (Ezekiel 34:12)
- God will __________ His sheep into their own land. (Ezekiel 34:13)
- God will __________ His sheep with good pasture. (Ezekiel 34:14)
- God will Himself __________ the shepherd of His sheep. (Ezekiel 34:15)
- God will make His sheep __________. (Ezekiel 34:15)
- God will __________ His lost sheep. (Ezekiel 34:16)

- God will bring __________ His strayed sheep. (Ezekiel 34:16)
- God will __________ His injured sheep. (Ezekiel 34:16)
- God will __________ His weak sheep. (Ezekiel 34:16)
- God will make a covenant of __________ with His sheep. (Ezekiel 34:25)
- God will make sure His sheep dwell ____________ in the wilderness. (Ezekiel 34:25)
- God will send down showers of _____________ for His sheep. (Ezekiel 34:26)
- God will ensure that none shall make His sheep ______________. (Ezekiel 34:28)
- God will ___________ for His sheep. (Ezekiel 34:29)

4. Reread the final verse of this chapter slowly, imagining that God is speaking to you.

   You are my sheep, human sheep of my pasture, and I am your God, declares the Lord God.
   EZEKIEL 34:31

5. Which promise from Ezekiel 34 do you need to cling to most? Write it down. I encourage you to work on memorizing it this week.

Joshua 21:45 tells us that none of the good promises of the Lord fail; all come to pass. With that in mind, read these promises again: God is seeking you out. God wants to rescue you and bring you into your own land—the good land He has for you. God wants to feed you the good things you need, and He Himself wants to shepherd you. God wants to make you lie down and give you the rest you need. He wants to bring you back to Himself and heal your wounds. God wants to strengthen you where you are weak and invite you into His covenant of peace. God wants you to dwell securely, and He wants to shower you with His specific blessings for your life in the appointed season. God wants to ensure that no one and nothing makes you afraid, and He wants to provide all your needs. Amen?

In chapter 5 of *So Much Better*, I talk about how our pain creates a hunger that is satisfied in the personhood of Jesus. What does that mean? It means He meets our every need . . . but until we are aware of our needs, we can't fully appreciate the way He meets them. Pain opens our eyes to our needs. Our areas of lack point us to the only One who fulfills our every need.

God is our healer, but we can't fully appreciate that until we've experienced our need for healing. God strengthens us, but we can't fully appreciate that until we are acquainted with our weakness. God gives us security, but we can't fully appreciate that until we've realized there is no true security in any of the other things we attempt to find it in. God is our provider, but we can't fully appreciate that until we feel the weight of our need for provision.

6. What area of need or lack in your life do you feel most strongly right now?

He meets our
every need . . .
but until we are
aware of our needs,
we can't fully
appreciate the way
He meets them.

7. How does God promise to meet that need?

8. Now let's take a look at John 10. In this passage, Jesus declares Himself the Good Shepherd and fulfills the prophecies of Ezekiel 34. Read verses 1-18 on your own. What do you notice in this passage about the relationship between the Good Shepherd and His sheep? Write down any observations that stand out to you.

John 10:3-5 says, "The sheep hear his voice, and he calls his own sheep by name and leads them out. When he has brought out all his own, he goes before them, and the sheep follow him, for they know his voice. A stranger they will not follow, but they will flee from him, for they do not know the voice of strangers." Imagine walking into a crowded room where a lot of people are talking. Now think of someone you're close to—maybe a spouse, a best friend, a parent, or a child. Would you be able to pick out that person's voice in the crowd? My guess is that you would. Why?

Because you know their voice. You've spent a lot of time with that person. You know what their voice sounds like, how they talk, what types of things they say. If someone else pretended to be this person, you wouldn't buy it because you would know it wasn't the voice of the person you know and love.

Jesus describes this type of intimacy with His sheep. He says that He calls His sheep by name and they know His voice. Quite often, it's in the pain and waiting that we press into God, read His Word, and pray—and that's when we develop a familiarity with what His voice sounds like.

9. How well do you feel like you know God's voice? Are there certain times His voice has been especially clear?

10. In the times when God's voice seems distant or unfamiliar, what practices can you implement to help you recognize it more?

John 10:10-11 says, "The thief comes only to steal and kill and destroy. I came that they may have life and have it abundantly. I am the good shepherd. The good shepherd lays down his life for the sheep." Abundant life doesn't necessarily denote an easy, comfortable, or picture-perfect life. Rather, it refers to a life of satisfaction in Jesus. This is available to us right here and now, not only on the other side of our waiting and pain. The enemy wants to steal, kill, and destroy, but Jesus wants to give us life . . . and He gave up His own life for us.

11. How has the enemy tried to steal, kill, and bring destruction to your life during this season?

12. In what ways do you see Jesus bringing you life right now, even amid difficult circumstances?

Psalm 34:18 says, "The Lord is near to the brokenhearted and saves the crushed in spirit." When you feel overwhelmed with heartache and pain, find comfort in the truth that God draws near to you in it. Ask Him to show you all the ways He is present and active in your life right now.

Prayer

Lord, show me that You are near to me in my areas of waiting and pain. Help me to keep my heart soft to You, even when time continues to pass with no change, even when I'm tempted to harden myself against You and distrust Your character. Show me any areas where I'm believing untrue things about You. Reveal Yourself to me and help me to see You clearly. Help me to cling to Your promises even when circumstances tempt me to think Your words aren't true. May this time be marked by increased intimacy with You and sensitivity to Your voice. In Jesus' name, amen.

Hide God's Word in Your Heart

Which key verse from this week's study stood out to you most? Highlight it and practice memorizing it this week.

> You are my sheep, human sheep of my pasture, and I am your God, declares the Lord God.
>
> **EZEKIEL 34:31**

> The thief comes only to steal and kill and destroy. I came that they may have life and have it abundantly. I am the good shepherd. The good shepherd lays down his life for the sheep.
>
> **JOHN 10:10-11**

> The LORD is near to the brokenhearted and saves the crushed in spirit.
> **PSALM 34:18**

Spend some time reflecting on what you learned in this study and what small step you can take toward applying it to your life this week.

VIDEO SESSION 3 NOTES

faith in the waiting

To access the video session, use the instructions in the front of your Bible study book.

journal entry of a modern-day widow of Zarephath

Faith in the Waiting

Inspired by 1 Kings 17:8-24

I don't know what I'm going to do. I don't see how You could possibly come through this time. Rent is due tomorrow. Do I send another text asking for help? I promised I wouldn't ask again—I thought things were finally looking up, that we wouldn't just be scraping by anymore. But then the day care rates went up. Unexpected car troubles cropped up. Anything else, Lord? It feels like nothing else could possibly go wrong. But I don't even want to say that, because then something else surely will.

I wish I could be like my daughter, blissfully unaware, enjoying a Happy Meal. I feel guilty I even bought it for her—I know it would have been cheaper and healthier to make food at home. But between working all day, rushing to pick her up, then taking the car in, it was the best I could do. And she was hungry. I'm doing my best, Lord. Why does it feel like I'm constantly failing and coming up short? Do You care for me like I care for her?

You say that You will provide for all our needs, and I believe that. At least, I really want to. But why does it feel like every day we're scraping the bottom of the barrel, trying to scrounge up just enough bread—sometimes literally?

I don't even know what I'm going to eat for dinner tonight—I just wanted to make sure there was enough for her. I'm so tired of living this way, Lord. Will we ever get to enter a Promised Land of plenty, or will it always be a wilderness of daily bread?

It seems like we can't catch a break, and sometimes it feels like You don't even care. Honestly, sometimes I just want to sit in that—like right now. But I'm speaking truth to my own heart. I'm feebly bringing to You the little bit of faith I have, and I'm asking You to multiply it. I don't see any feasible scenario where things could be different than they are now. Where we could be doing something other than living paycheck to paycheck. But I know You see things that I don't see. I want to honor You with my finances, Lord. I want to provide a good life for my little girl. And I know that faith is being sure of what we hope for and certain of what we cannot see. I can't see a path forward, but I'm certain of Your character—that You are all-powerful. You made the heavens and the earth; nothing is too hard for You.

Help me to trust You, Lord. Take my little bit of faith and grow it. Take my handful of flour and my little bit of oil in the jug, and keep them full every day with what we need. May You fill them abundantly—and may they never run out.

SESSION 3

faith in the waiting

To get the most out of this week's study, read chapters 8–11 of So Much Better.

I used to work in communications for a power company, and one time as a sort of field trip, we visited a power plant that uses ocean water to generate electricity. During the tour, I was spellbound by the many sounds. I could faintly hear the waves rolling in and seagulls squawking enthusiastically overhead. Inside, machines whirred thunderously as they worked to accomplish their tasks. With the high pitches and low rumbles, it was a symphony of productivity. We went from room to room, until we finally entered one so loud earplugs were required. I squished mine in, then stepped forward. A dungeon-like door slammed behind us, and a new world opened in front.

With my earplugs in place, my focus shifted. I could no longer hear the faint waves or the seagulls, and the deafening mechanical sounds were now replaced by a muted droning. Instead, my attention was drawn inward, and I was suddenly aware of everything happening in me. My heartbeat rang loudly in my ears, and each step I took resounded like the beat of a drum. I was tuned in to each breath, and even my thoughts seemed more prominent, more clear. It's as if the removal of one of my senses—external hearing—made me acutely aware of what was happening within.

I think God sometimes does something similar through our waiting. Only it's generally not our sense of hearing He obstructs but our sense of sight. We want to know the what and the when and the who and the how and the where of His plan, but most of the time, He doesn't give us that information ahead of time. Unable to rely on our own sense of sight, we're forced to rely on something else instead: God's unchanging character.

Hebrews 11:1 says, "Now faith is being sure of what we hope for and certain of what we do not see" (NIV). By simple logic, this means that when we're walking by faith, there's a lot about God's plan for our lives we won't be able to see. While we wait for His plan to unfold, He invites us to strengthen our faith.

In chapter 8 of *So Much Better*, I talk about how Abraham was seventy-five years old when God first gave him the promise that he would become the father of a great nation (see Genesis 12). If I were him, I would have assumed it was going to happen soon. Maybe Abraham did too. Maybe he rushed home, all excited, to tell Sarah, and the two of them started dreaming up baby names and planning the nursery. But then a year went by and nothing happened. Years turned into decades, and they were still waiting. They started to wonder, *Did we hear God wrong?*

In the Bible, we see that when God gives a vision or a promise, He often gives it because He knows darkness is coming—a vast stretch of wilderness where we won't be able to see a thing. In giving us the revelation ahead of time, God is offering us an opportunity to build our faith by holding on to His Word just as our circumstances are about to shift, making the fulfillment of His Word feel impossible.

1. Is there a promise you believe God has spoken over your life that you're waiting on Him to fulfill?

One of the hardest parts of waiting is not knowing if we should keep waiting on God and praying for the thing we desire or if the fact that He hasn't given it to us yet is an indication that it isn't something He has for us. The heart question is not only *How do I persist in prayer?* but also *Should I persist in prayer . . . or should I let it go?*

The thing is, there are concrete promises found in God's Word that we can take to the bank and *know* He will fulfill:

- He will always be with us (see Isaiah 41:10).
- He will keep us in perfect peace when we keep our minds fixed on Him (see Isaiah 26:3).
- He will show us the way we should go (see Psalm 32:8).
- He will use the trials we walk through to produce steadfastness in us (see James 1:2-4).
- When we resist the enemy, he will flee from us (see James 4:7).
- He will supply all our needs (see Philippians 4:19).

These are a mere six of the 7,487 promises God makes directly to humankind in His Word! But the specifics of how He'll fulfill those promises? Or whether certain desires of ours—like marriage, motherhood, material things, or a particular milestone—will be fulfilled? Those are things we aren't promised in Scripture. We know that God cares about our desires, but we don't have a guarantee that every desire we have in this lifetime will be fulfilled. How, then, can we know if God intends to give us what we desire or if we're waiting for something that isn't going to happen? This is another area where, with our inability to see ahead, we have the opportunity to build our faith.

2. Read Philippians 4:6-7 (ESV) and fill in the blanks:

   Do not be anxious about ______________, but in ____________ by ___________ and supplication with ________________ let your requests be made known to God. And the ______________ of God, which surpasses all understanding, will guard your hearts and your minds in Christ Jesus.

As I talk about in chapter 13 of *So Much Better*, if a desire is on your heart, there are really only three options for what to do with it: You can pray about it, you can worry about it, or you can try to put it out of your mind altogether.

Worrying isn't really an option, at least not biblically. God tells us not to worry! And putting it out of our minds isn't a very effective strategy when it's something we really want. But we can pray about everything—this is not only a biblical option but a command! God tells us to pray with thanksgiving—telling Him what we need while thanking Him for everything He has done. This gives us a lens of gratitude to look through and keeps us from obsessing over our desires as we bring them before Him. When we thank God for all He is already doing, it creates a heart posture of trust by reminding us of His good character even while we wait.

3. Which of these options do you tend to gravitate toward when it comes to the thing you desire: praying about it, worrying about it, or trying to put it out of your mind?

4. When do you find it especially difficult to pray about the thing you're waiting for? Why do you think that is?

5. God is working good in our lives even while we wait—and He tells us to thank Him for that good so we can experience His peace. What good do you see God working in your life right now?

It can be wearying to keep praying for something when you see no change, but remaining persistent in prayer is better than the alternative. When we try to numb ourselves to the desires of our hearts, we miss the opportunity to vulnerably bring them before Him and then see Him work in our hearts. Prayer is powerful, and prayer changes things—whether that's the situation we're praying about or whether it's us. Oftentimes it's both.

6. Look up Psalm 37:4 (ESV) and fill in the missing word: "______________ yourself in the LORD, and he will give you the desires of your heart."

This is one of those verses we often get wrong. We take it to mean, "Find joy in God, and He will give you whatever you want." But neither Scripture nor reality supports that interpretation. So what does it actually mean?

In chapter 8 of *So Much Better*, we talk about how in the original Hebrew, the word translated as *delight* means "to be soft and pliable" in the hands of God.[1] Psalm 37:4 doesn't mean that God is our genie and if we tell Him what we want, He will magically give it to us. This isn't a blank check to cash in for the perfect husband or

[1] "6026. Anog," Bible Hub, accessed July 31, 2025, https://biblehub.com/hebrew/6026.htm.

Prayer is powerful, and prayer changes things—whether that's the situation we're praying about or whether it's us. Oftentimes it's both.

the beautiful mansion or the dream job or the exact number of children we've always hoped to have. Rather, it means that as we are in intimate relationship with God and delight in His character, over time He will change our desires and affections so they align with His perfect will for us. He will *give* us the desires of our hearts, meaning He will put *His* desires into us. How mind-blowing is that? To delight ourselves in the Lord essentially means to grow in knowledge of who He is and in love for Him, to the point that we die to ourselves and submit ourselves to the Lord because we know He is better and His ways are better . . . even if they're different from our own (which they usually are).

Think of Sarah. God's plans for her were good, and if you know how her story ends, you know how much bigger they were than anything she could have dreamed up on her own. Sarah wanted a single baby, but God wanted to birth through her an entire *nation*. Still, even though God's plans are so much better than ours, letting go of our own plans can feel painful, especially if this involves the death of a dream. Maybe you never imagined being at this stage in your life while still waiting for certain things . . . just like I'm sure Sarah never imagined having her first child at ninety. It's okay to bring that hurt before God. Necessary, even. I encourage you to do so.

7. Take some time to tell God how you're feeling about the waiting, the grief of a lost timeline, or the deferment of a dream. Ask Him to show you that He sees you and ask Him to help you trust that His plans for you are good.

8. Now read this verse slowly. According to the text, how did Abraham strengthen his faith while waiting in the dark?

   No unbelief made [Abraham] waver concerning the promise of God, but he grew strong in his faith as he gave glory to God, fully convinced that God was able to do what he had promised.
   ROMANS 4:20-21

What does it mean to give glory to God? It means we see Him for who He truly is and acknowledge His goodness. In other words, when we fix our gaze on God's character and fill our minds and hearts with worship for who He is, it builds our faith, even as we wander in the darkness.

9. Following is a list of some of God's attributes. Circle a few you need to focus on in this season and spend some time meditating on them.

   - God is *eternal*.

     You, O LORD, are enthroned forever; you are remembered throughout all generations.
     PSALM 102:12

   - God is *good*.

     Good and upright is the LORD; therefore he instructs sinners in the way.
     PSALM 25:8

- God is *gracious.*

Gracious is the LORD, and righteous; our God is merciful.
PSALM 116:5

- God is *holy.*

There is none holy like the LORD: for there is none besides you; there is no rock like our God.
1 SAMUEL 2:2

- God is *immanent* (ever-present).

Behold, I am with you always, to the end of the age.
MATTHEW 28:20

- God is *immutable* (unchanging).

I the LORD do not change.
MALACHI 3:6

- God is *just.*

The LORD is a God of justice; blessed are all those who wait for him.
ISAIAH 30:18

- God is *loving.*

The steadfast love of the LORD never ceases; his mercies never come to an end; they are new every morning; great is your faithfulness.
LAMENTATIONS 3:22-23

- God is *omnipotent* (all-powerful).

Ah, Lord GOD! It is you who have made the heavens and the earth by your great power and by your outstretched arm! Nothing is too hard for you.
JEREMIAH 32:17

- God is *omnipresent* (all-present).

Can a man hide himself in secret places so that I cannot see him? declares the LORD. Do I not fill heaven and earth? declares the LORD.
JEREMIAH 23:24

- God is *sovereign* (in control over all things).

We know that for those who love God all things work together for good, for those who are called according to his purpose.
ROMANS 8:28

Prayer

Lord, I know that You see the desires of my heart. Even though I can't see Your plans for me, help me to fix my gaze on Your character. Show me who You are. Reveal Yourself to me as I spend time with You and read Your Word. Help me to truly delight in You. Strengthen my faith as I fix my eyes on who You are. Help me to walk by faith even when I can't see, and help me to trust that Your plans for me are good, even if they're different from my own. In Jesus' name, amen.

Hide God's Word in Your Heart

Which key verse from this week's study stood out to you most? Highlight it and practice memorizing it this week.

> Faith is being sure of what we hope for and certain of what we do not see.
> **HEBREWS 11:1, NIV**

> Do not be anxious about anything, but in everything by prayer and supplication with thanksgiving let your requests be made known to God.

And the peace of God, which surpasses all understanding, will guard your hearts and your minds in Christ Jesus.
PHILIPPIANS 4:6-7

Delight yourself in the LORD, and he will give you the desires of your heart.
PSALM 37:4

Spend some time reflecting on what you learned in this study and what small step you can take toward applying it to your life this week.

VIDEO SESSION 4 NOTES

humility in the waiting

To access the video session, use the instructions in the front of your Bible study book.

journal entry of a modern-day mother of a prodigal

Humility in the Waiting

Inspired by Luke 15:11-32

I got a call from the police station tonight. When I first answered, I was so afraid I could barely breathe. He used his one call to tell me what had happened—they found some stuff on him he shouldn't have had, and now he'll be spending the night behind bars. I'm relieved to know he's physically safe, of course. But my heart feels like it's tearing in two.

How did we get here, Lord? Where did we go wrong? We read him the Bible stories, took him to church, did our best to teach him Your ways. "Train up a child in the way he should go; even when he is old he will not depart from it." I turned to that verse again and again during the training years. But despite all our efforts, he did depart from the way we trained him. And now my heart is breaking every day as I watch him destroy his body, ruin his mind, and throw his life away.

I never thought this would be our story, Lord. I thought he would be serving You, maybe married by now to a lovely woman who loves and fears You. I thought I would be on the brink of having grandchildren to enjoy and love and pray for. Instead, I'm praying every day that You would spare his life. I'm sure the other ladies at church will talk, but I don't even care anymore. I care about him. Years of sacrifice and lovingly pouring into him, only to watch him squander it all on reckless living. Oh Lord, that he would only see how empty that way of life is! That he would only come to the end of himself and turn back to You.

I don't know why this is happening, Lord, or why You're allowing it. I know You don't owe me an answer, and I know I probably wouldn't understand even if You did give me one—because I would never choose this for him myself. But I do know that You promise to work all things for the good of those who love You—even this, even though it doesn't seem good in any way. I know that Your purposes in his story are bigger than I can see in this moment, for Your ways are not my ways and Your thoughts are not my thoughts. Help me to trust You, Lord. I am helpless to bring about any change in his heart, but I know that even a king's heart is a stream of water in Your hand.

Lord, I know that You can turn this into a powerful testimony in his life that speaks of Your plentiful redemption. And I'll never stop hoping or praying for that until the day I take my last breath. Seek after him, Lord. Soften his heart by Your love and kindness and grace. Speak to him in unmistakable ways; remind him of Your truth. I long for the day when I can see him turn to You and melt into Your welcoming embrace, even when he's still a long way off. I long to celebrate his return.

SESSION 4

humility in the waiting

To get the most out of this week's study, read chapters 12–15 of So Much Better.

Can I confess something? Sometimes I think I'm entitled to judge how God does or does not respond in a particular situation and determine whether His actions (or lack thereof) are just. Of course, I don't *actually* believe I have any authority to judge God's actions—and when I admit this out loud, I realize how heretical it sounds. But if I'm being honest, sometimes I operate as if this is exactly what I believe.

Now, before you judge me, I invite you to reflect a bit. Maybe, just maybe, you can relate?

When you've been praying for something for a long time, have you ever been tempted to feel like it's not fair that God has answered this prayer for so many people around you but not for you? Have you even been tempted to feel like you've done more to deserve having your prayer answered than those who are actually getting it answered . . . as icky as that may be to admit?

I have.

Or maybe you thought God was in something—perhaps an answer to a long-awaited prayer or something new and hopeful in your life. But then things don't turn out at all how you imagined. Maybe they even go horribly wrong. What you thought was a beautiful answer to prayer is now a painful disappointment, an area in need of healing. You're tempted to feel like it wasn't right of God to allow you to walk through that, only to have it turn out the way it did. Why would a good God who loves you let that happen? Have you ever felt this way?

I have as well.

In chapter 14 of *So Much Better*, I share how I thought God was finally answering a deep heart prayer of mine, only to give me (quite literally) a front-row seat to watch Him give it to someone else instead. I was hurt and confused. I had been so sure that God was in this situation . . . so why would He allow it to turn out this way? As I searched for any good God was bringing from a hard situation, He exposed something ugly in my heart. I wasn't merely trying to see the positive side of things; I was trying to weigh whether enough good would come of this to justify God for allowing it to happen at all.

Whoa. Who am I to make myself the judge over God's actions?

Though it seemed like maybe the waiting was finally coming to an end, it turned out that God still had more good work to do in the waiting: He was using it to humble me.

About halfway through the Bible, we find the book of Job. It's about a man named Job who was wealthy and had lots of kids. But God allowed everything to be taken from him in the blink of an eye. As Job grappled with all this, lots of well-meaning people said unhelpful things. But God used one man named Elihu to bring Job a little nugget of wisdom.

1. Read Job 35:1-16 slowly. Write down some of the key phrases that stand out to you.

2. What do you think is the heart of what Elihu is saying to Job?

Elihu had some questions for Job as Job grappled with the pain and destruction God had allowed in his life. Elihu challenged the idea that because Job was a righteous man, he deserved only good from God. Elihu also challenged the idea, presented by Job's friends, that Job's suffering must be the result of sin.

3. Do you believe that if you do good, you deserve good from God?

4. Do you believe that any bad things that happen in your life must be the result of your sin?

5. Read Job 1:1 and circle all the words and phrases used to describe Job:

   There was a man in the land of Uz whose name was Job, and that man was blameless and upright, one who feared God and turned away from evil.

6. Job is described as blameless and upright—someone who feared God and resisted evil. How does this challenge the idea that if we do good, we deserve good, and that anything bad in our lives is the result of our sin?

Both of these ideas are faulty theology: that if we do good, we deserve good, and that if we do bad, we deserve bad. That's not how God works. Scripture says that even our righteousness is "filthy rags" (Isaiah 64:6, NIV), and Jesus makes clear in John 9 that not all ailments we experience in this life are a result of our sin. Sometimes things do or don't happen for reasons God has not granted us to know, but we do know that in all things He is manifesting His glory.

Elihu also raised the issue of entitlement (see Job 35). He said that we don't hear an answer from God when we feel like we're entitled to an explanation from Him simply because we don't see or understand what He is doing.

7. When have you felt that God owed you an explanation for what was happening (or not happening) in your life? Take some time to reflect honestly before God.

Unbeknownst to Job, Elihu, or any of his friends, Job's circumstances on earth were brought about by a conversation between God and Satan in heaven. Satan knew that God had blessed Job's life immensely, and Satan wanted to test Job to see if he would still love and worship God even if everything was taken away from him. Satan's hypothesis was that he wouldn't. God allowed the test, and that's when all the bad stuff in Job's life went down.

While Job was trying to figure out why things were happening in his life, God had a bigger purpose in all of it than Job could see or know. God had made the actual *why* answer unknowable to Job. And this is precisely the point of the book of Job: We can't always know the reason God allows certain things to happen, and His goodness isn't dependent on Him offering one.

8. **Read through this verse slowly:**

> My thoughts are not your thoughts, neither are your ways my ways, declares the LORD. For as the heavens are higher than the earth, so are my ways higher than your ways and my thoughts than your thoughts.
> **ISAIAH 55:8-9**

Now copy it down, meditating on each word as you write:

Through his wrestling with God, Job was brought to the end of himself, and he was humbled. God often uses waiting seasons to accomplish the same end in us—stripping us of our sense of entitlement and teaching us to trust Him even when we don't understand. This is a theme we see all throughout Scripture: God uses the waiting to create humility in the hearts of His people.

9. **Look up Deuteronomy 8:2-3 (ESV) and fill in the blanks:**

You shall remember the whole way that the LORD your God has led you these forty years in the wilderness, that he might ________________ you, testing you to know what was in your heart, whether you would keep his commandments or not. And he ________________ you and let you hunger and fed you with manna, which you did not know, nor did your fathers know, that he might make you know that man does not live by bread alone, but man lives by every word that comes from the mouth of the LORD.

10. **What does this passage tell us was one of God's big purposes for the Israelites in their time of waiting and wandering in the wilderness?**

God often uses our waiting seasons and the hard things that happen to humble us and make us wholly dependent on Him. That's not to say He uses the waiting to punish us for being prideful. But it is to say that His timing is perfect—and before bringing us into the next new thing, He has a good purpose for exactly where we are. God uses the waiting to expose our sense of entitlement—thinking we have a right to understand everything He does—and to bring us to a place of simply trusting Him.

When God finally answered Job toward the end of the book, He didn't open by explaining the exchange between Himself and Satan. He could have, but He didn't—and to our knowledge, Job never found out. God never gave Job any explanation for the circumstances of his suffering. Instead, in a thunderous, glorious monologue, God revealed to Job who He is: eternal, sovereign, majestic, all-powerful, wise, perfect. The simple implication: God is God. Job is not.

11. Read Job 38–40:2. What are your impressions of God from this passage? Write down any observations that stand out to you.

12. As you think through this passage, spend some time reflecting on your own life. Who have you seen God to be in your waiting?

The story of Job shows us that it's okay to ask God questions about why things are (or aren't) happening in our lives. But it also warns that we might not get an answer—or even be able to understand it if we do. God is sovereign over every process in the universe and over every tiny detail that unfolds in our lives. His wisdom is unsearchable. God doesn't owe us an answer . . . but He does invite us to trust His character even when we can't see His hand.

13. Read Job 42:10:

> The LORD restored the fortunes of Job, when he had prayed for his friends. And the LORD gave Job twice as much as he had before.

God promises to work good out of not-good situations, not because He owes it to us but because that's who He is.

Look up the definition of the word *restore* in a dictionary and write it here:

Hearing how Job's story ends makes me think of 1 Peter 5:10. This is God's promise to us in whatever we walk through. Read through it slowly:

> After you have suffered a little while, the God of all grace, who has called you to his eternal glory in Christ, will himself restore, confirm, strengthen, and establish you.

God didn't owe Job a double blessing. Even if He hadn't changed Job's circumstances, He would still be good. Yet God did restore Job, because that's who He is. And we have this same promise in God's character. God doesn't owe us a single thing, yet in His goodness and faithfulness, He promises to work all things together for the good of those who love Him—even when things don't make sense, even if we never get the why question answered. God promises to work good out of not-good situations, not because He owes it to us but because that's who He is.

14. Read these two verses slowly:

> We know that for those who love God all things work together for good, for those who are called according to his purpose.
> **ROMANS 8:28**

> In this you rejoice, though now for a little while, if necessary, you have been grieved by various trials, so that the tested genuineness of your faith—more precious than gold that perishes though it is tested by fire—may be found to result in praise and glory and honor at the revelation of Jesus Christ.
> **1 PETER 1:6-7**

According to 1 Peter 1:6-7, how can we know our faith is genuine?

15. According to 1 Peter 1:6-7, when our faith is found to be genuine, what does this result in?

16. Have you found that your faith has grown through waiting or other trials? In what ways?

Prayer

Lord, show me how You are using my waiting to create in me a heart of humility. Expose any areas of entitlement or ways I am relying on my own understanding, strength, or ability rather than on You. Help me to trust You even when I don't understand what You are doing, and use this waiting time to deepen my faith. Help me to be faithful to You even when things don't go the way I hoped. I pray that in Your perfect timing, You would heal, restore, confirm, strengthen, and establish me—and that You would lead me into the next new thing You have for me. I know Your plans and purposes are good. Reveal to me the good work You are doing in me even while I wait. In Jesus' name, amen.

Hide God's Word in Your Heart

Which key verse from this week's study stood out to you most? Highlight it and practice memorizing it this week.

> My thoughts are not your thoughts, neither are your ways my ways, declares the LORD. For as the heavens are higher than the earth, so are my ways higher than your ways and my thoughts than your thoughts.
> **ISAIAH 55:8-9**

> We know that for those who love God all things work together for good, for those who are called according to his purpose.
> **ROMANS 8:28**

> In this you rejoice, though now for a little while, if necessary, you have been grieved by various trials, so that the tested genuineness of your faith—more precious than gold that perishes though it is tested by fire—may be found to result in praise and glory and honor at the revelation of Jesus Christ.
> **1 PETER 1:6-7**

Spend some time reflecting on what you learned in this study and what small step you can take toward applying it to your life this week.

VIDEO SESSION 5 NOTES

fruitfulness in the waiting

To access the video session, use the instructions in the front of your Bible study book.

journal entry of a modern-day Anna

Fruitfulness in the Waiting

Inspired by Luke 2:36-38

Here I am spending another evening in the stillness of my small apartment, gearing up for a big day tomorrow. Not my *big day, of course, someone else's—again. Now, Lord, I'm asking You to prep my heart for yet another day spent at yet another wedding, when all I long for is to become a wife myself.*

I never imagined I'd be well into my thirties with no prospect of a godly husband in sight. I never imagined I'd watch my best friends celebrate their ten-year wedding anniversaries while I'm still in the middle of a decades-long wait myself. I never imagined I'd visit my sister and her three kids, with their joyful chaos and kitchen floor strewed with rogue toys and Cheerios . . . only to return home to my own floors, which are painfully clean. My single "season" is starting to feel more like a lifelong commitment—only it's not the one I wanted to make. Are You truly able to do immeasurably more than anything I could think to ask for or imagine, Lord? Or is that only true for everyone else?

My life isn't full the way I imagined it would be at this age, but it isn't empty either. Amid my sadness, I've asked for eyes to see what You have for me here and now. Like Anna, You've asked me to simply dwell in Your presence and offer myself for Your service. So I started a small group with other women in my church who are also feeling out of place. I've been intentional to check in on and care for my aging parents. I've volunteered to serve and signed up for missions opportunities. And I've been amazed at the ways You've used me—and also blessed me—through these things. You've shown me that my waiting isn't wasted. Though I feel stripped-down in many ways, I see undeniable fruit.

Some days I'm able to see the good parts of a life I wouldn't have chosen, and I'm able to celebrate with other people who are getting the gift I long for. But other days I need a little assurance, Lord: Do You still see me*?*

I know You know my heart, Lord. You know my desires, and You know my soul-weariness. Help me to remain in You, Lord, even when I'm mad at You. Help me to bring my raw emotions before You when it would be easier to numb them out. Help me to stay soft to Your Spirit, even when the pain tempts me to harden my heart. Help me to trust that for everything You've taken away, You're preparing something better to take its place. Help me to believe that You aren't withholding, but protecting—and preserving for me Your very best.

SESSION 5

fruitfulness in the waiting

To get the most out of this week's study, read chapters 16–18 of So Much Better.

There's an underrated skill I'm convinced should be an Olympic sport. If it were, I wouldn't even make it on the medal stand. The skill: trimming a squirmy baby's fingernails. (Putting a bow in a wiggly baby girl's hair falls under the same category, but I digress.)

It's a bit easier now that he's a toddler, but when my firstborn was a baby, he couldn't stand having his fingernails cut. This was especially true once he learned to crawl—he was a busy boy who had things to do, people to see, and Tupperware drawers to empty. Sitting still for ten minutes so mama could complete this dreaded but necessary task? Hard pass. He'd rather eat last night's chicken that he chucked on the floor.

The problem is, I can't simply let the task of trimming fingernails slide, no matter how much my babies don't like it. If I do, they'll end up scratching themselves. I know, because it's happened before. If their nails grow too long, it will also be harder for them to practice their fine motor skills—like turning the pages of their favorite picture book or grasping a beloved puff. So as they try to squirm away and sometimes cry while I cut their nails, I tell them, "I know you don't like this, baby, but Mama has to do it, or else you'll hurt yourself."

Isn't this God's heart when He's pruning us? We don't like it because it's uncomfortable—even painful—and because we feel like it slows us down and keeps us from doing the things we want to do. Yet God knows that unless He cuts certain things away, we won't be able to grow, we'll be limited in the good works we can do, and the very things that should have been trimmed away will end up hurting us.

As we talked about in chapter 16 of *So Much Better*, God prunes because of His love for us and His desire to see us bear fruit. We don't always know why He allows us to go through long seasons of waiting or other situations that seem to strip us bare. But we do have the promise that He will always be with us in the things we walk through and that He will always work good from them. He will use our waiting seasons to produce in us the fruit of greater growth into the likeness of Christ and maturity of faith.

1. **Read John 15:1-11 slowly. What words are repeated often? Write them down, along with any other observations you have from the text as you read.**

To give a bit of context for this passage, John 15 is capturing an intimate time of Jesus teaching His disciples and giving promises to them (and us) right before He was crucified. If you think about the last words a person shares as they're dying, you instinctively know they're important since this is what that person wants to leave you with. Jesus wanted His disciples, including you and me, to know how important it is to abide in Him. Since we know this was important to Jesus, we need to first figure out what it means.

2. Look up the definition of the word *abide* in the dictionary and write it down.

To abide is to accept or act in accordance with; to stay or to remain.

Think of your car. Beyond its obvious purpose of getting you from point A to point B, many cars have a whole slew of other capabilities: navigation, lane departure warning, connectivity to your phone, automatic emergency braking, and start-stop technology to save fuel. Some cars can even park or drive themselves! But in order for a car to do any of these things, there's one thing it needs: energy. Without access to the aforementioned fuel or to a charging station (I see you, EV drivers), this complex automobile is utterly useless. Apart from a power source, a car is nothing more than a clunky piece of metal.

The same is true for you and me spiritually. Ephesians 2:10 says,

> We are his workmanship, created in Christ Jesus for good works, which God prepared beforehand, that we should walk in them.

3. What do you think it means to be God's "workmanship"?

Each of us is fearfully and wonderfully made, with a purpose: to bear fruit for God's glory and our good. With God's Spirit in us, we have the ability to produce the fruit talked about in Galatians 5:22-23: love, joy, peace, patience, kindness, goodness, faithfulness, gentleness, and self-control. We were created to walk in the good works God prepared for each of us to do for His Kingdom. But apart from our power source, Jesus, we can do nothing.

Jesus tells us this plainly. Trying to do anything good apart from Jesus is like cutting a branch off a rosebush and willing it to grow a rosebud on its own. It's like trying to tape a half-grown fruit back onto its tree in hopes that it will grow to maturity—it simply isn't going to happen. A rose branch or a fruit bud can only produce the growth it was intended to produce when it's connected to its source.

4. God often uses our waiting seasons to help us bear rich fruit in our lives. How, exactly, does this work? Read what Jesus says in John 15:2 and write it below:

What is pruning? To prune is to cut away the dead or overgrown parts of a plant to increase its fruitfulness and growth. If you've ever used garden shears, you know they're sharp. This means that the pruning process often feels painful for the plant. In pruning us, God cuts things out of our lives—maybe certain relationships, bad habits, old mindsets, or our attachment to the plans and timelines we had in mind for how our lives were supposed to go. But as painful as this process is, it's the only way to grow.

5. What do you sense God pruning from your life in your current season?

When our prayers don't get answered the way we hoped, when God cuts things out of our lives, or when we experience something painful, it's easy to think we're being punished for something. But according to this verse, pruning doesn't mean we're doing something wrong. It might actually mean we're doing something *right*.

6. Take a look at John 15:2 again. What does Jesus say will happen to the branches that do not bear fruit?

Pruning is an indication God is preparing you to bear more fruit.

7. What does He say will happen to the branches that do bear fruit?

Jesus says that the branches with no fruit are taken away. But the branches that do have fruit are pruned . . . so they will bear more fruit. What does this mean? It means that pruning does not equal punishment; rather, pruning is an indication God is preparing you to bear more fruit.

This isn't to say that every hard circumstance is pruning. Sometimes difficulties in our lives are the result of our own poor choices (e.g., if you're failing a class because you never show up or do the homework). It's also not to say that God can't redeem our poor choices—because He absolutely can and does. The point is that we don't always do something to cause the negative things that happen in our lives.

Let's remember the first part of the definition of *abide*: "to accept or act in accordance with." If you're continually reading God's Word, accepting it as truth, applying it to your life, and repenting of any sin God reveals through it, then it's likely the hard things in your life aren't the result of your actions. Yet sometimes God allows hard things to happen, and He will use those things to refine us—to trim our dead or unnecessary parts so we look more like Jesus.

8. How have your trials or waiting seasons made you more desperate for God?

9. How has God produced fruit and growth in your life through pruning in the past? How might He be bringing good things from your current season as well?

10. Take a look at John 15:8. According to Jesus, what is fruit in our lives evidence of?

11. Now take a look at John 15:11. What is Jesus' hope for us as we abide in Him and bear fruit?

Jesus tells us to abide in Him not just to give us another thing to do. He tells us to abide in Him because He knows that staying connected to Him and bearing fruit for His glory is the only way we can experience true joy.

True joy isn't found in a certain set of circumstances but in Christ alone. And it's not only found on the other side of our waiting but in the here and now. That's not to say God doesn't care about the desires of our hearts—He does. But God knows that nothing can truly satisfy us apart from Himself.

12. Here are five ways we can abide in Jesus throughout our everyday lives. Circle one area you'd like to focus on this week. In the blank after it, write down specifically where and when and how you could put this into practice.

Prayer

____

Reading the Bible

____

Connecting with Christian community

____

Consuming content that draws you closer to God (and avoiding content that doesn't)

____

Worship

____

James 4:8 says, "Draw near to God, and he will draw near to you." We can be encouraged knowing that abiding in Him isn't all on us—God is ultimately the One drawing us closer to His heart.

13. What are some habits or practices that help you draw closer to Jesus?

14. What are some things that pull you away from Jesus?

15. Spend some time reflecting on and praying through your answers to these questions and ask God what changes He might be leading you to make to help you abide in Him more.

As you wait on God, remember that the results are up to Him but the obedience is up to you. As we talked about in chapter 16 of *So Much Better*, when God told Noah that a worldwide flood was coming and instructed him to build an ark, Noah's job wasn't to figure out when the rain would start or to worry about whether it actually would or to convince people it was coming when all they could see was a clear sky. Noah's job was simply to put his head down and get to work in faithful obedience.

16. What is the next right step you sense God asking you to take while you wait on Him?

Prayer

Lord, thank You that pruning doesn't mean I'm being punished. Rather, it means there's fruit in my life and You intend for me to bear even more fruit. Show me how You are growing me in the waiting, and help me to grow into who You created me to be and walk in the purposes You have for my life. Help me to abide in You and act in accordance with Your Word. Show me any areas of my life that are not in alignment with Your Word and bring me into alignment with You. Help me to abide in You day by day, moment by moment, and to bear much fruit for Your glory and my good. May I look back on this season as one where You did significant work in me—a season that bore the sweetest fruit. In Jesus' name, amen.

Hide God's Word in Your Heart

Which key verse from this week's study stood out to you most? Highlight it and practice memorizing it this week.

> Every branch in me that does not bear fruit he takes away, and every branch that does bear fruit he prunes, that it may bear more fruit.
> **JOHN 15:2**

> We are his workmanship, created in Christ Jesus for good works, which God prepared beforehand, that we should walk in them.
> **EPHESIANS 2:10**

> Draw near to God, and he will draw near to you.
> **JAMES 4:8**

Spend some time reflecting on what you learned in this study and what small step you can take toward applying it to your life this week.

VIDEO SESSION 6 NOTES

transformation in the waiting

To access the video session, use the instructions in the front of your Bible study book.

journal entry of a modern-day Naomi

Transformation in the Waiting

Inspired by Ruth 1

It happened again. I was tapping through Instagram stories when I saw the post. They hung out again, and I wasn't invited. Seriously, Lord, what gives?

It always seems to hit me most on the slow days. With two under two, most days are pretty full—we have errands to run, playdates to get to. Then there's the car ride home, when I frantically try to keep them awake so that a five-minute car snooze doesn't ruin their two-hour crib nap. And, of course, laundry and dishes, the constant messes that need cleaning—I do my best to keep up with everything, all while trying to stay present with these little blessings I love more than anything.

But on a day like today, when we have no real plans, I wish more than anything I could text a best friend to come over and sip coffee with me while our kids play. We have community here, of course. But there's nothing like an old friend—someone you have history with, who you can effortlessly have heart conversations with, who you don't have to be "on" with. Friendships look different as a mama. And when you move to a new place while pregnant with your first, not only do you have to start over, you have to start over while navigating an entirely new season.

I think when you move from the place you grew up in and the people you love scatter too, it's hard for any one place to feel fully like home. Because bits of your heart—best friends, family members—now live all across the map. Sure, you can return to your geographical home, but it won't be home in the same way anymore, because the people you love are no longer there.

Lord, I know You see the desires of my heart, and I know You care. The answered prayers I'm living in now are evidence of that. This is the most joyful and fulfilling chapter I've lived yet, and I wouldn't trade it for the world. Home is wherever this little family You've given me is. But when it comes to friendship, I sometimes feel alone.

I'm tempted to dream of a day when I will have friends nearby with solid, deep roots. And I trust that day will come. In Your perfect timing, God, You take our areas of bitter longing and grief and turn them into places of pleasant delight. But it's a trap to get caught up waiting for that day, because then I will miss the gift of now. And only You know what new longings or unknown pain points will spring up in my life even when that day comes.

Perhaps the goal isn't to wait for the day when I'm no longer waiting for something—because this side of eternity, that day will never come. Instead, Lord, will You show me what You're doing in *my wait? And will You use this longing to remind me that heaven alone is my true home?*

SESSION 6

transformation in the waiting

To get the most out of this week's study, read chapters 19–21 of So Much Better.

Let me tell you about one of the coolest days I've ever experienced. It was during my trip to Iceland during the summer, when the sun never truly sets. At that time of year, there are twenty-four hours of sunlight in Iceland, which means you're able to pack a *lot* of sightseeing into a single day. On that particular day, my friend and I frolicked through fields of lupine flowers, felt the mist of the enormous Skógafoss waterfall, watched paragliders peek over clifftops against a purple sky, climbed a hilltop backlit by a cotton candy sky, and got a glimpse of Jökulsárlón, otherwise known as the breathtaking Glacier Lagoon.

"THIS IS THE COOLEST THING I'VE EVER SEEN!" I yelled when I saw it. I couldn't help it. That's what happens when your eyes meet glory—it comes gushing out of you.

In reflecting on the day and trying to understand why it felt so magical, my mind went immediately to the twenty-four-hour sun. This northern phenomenon allowed our day to stretch out, and the longer it got, the more dreamlike it started to feel. It wasn't simply that the day held cool moments. It was that the day had become an unending string of cool moments wrapped in one long, uninterrupted highlight reel. Each new wonder compounded on the next, making every moment more incredible than the one before. The day was cool because of each of the individual experiences, but it was the *coolest* because of all the experiences together—because it was so *full*. It was as if God poured out goodness on us so relentlessly, it was overwhelming. We couldn't quite hold it all in.

And I think that's a little bit like how heaven will be.

Here on earth, we experience God's glory as it pokes through the pains of a broken and fallen world. In heaven, we'll experience it uninterrupted and full.

Think of every happy memory, every sight that has ever captivated you, every moment of pure, unadulterated joy. Here on earth, these events pop up sporadically amid mundane, painful, or sad moments . . . because that's life—good and bad, happy and hard all rolled up into one. But we have the promise of a day when it will be *only* good because we'll be fully restored to right relationship with God. Think of all your most joyful moments, coming at you uninterrupted, almost overwhelming you with their sheer relentlessness. Even that is only a glimpse of the sure hope we have as followers of Jesus. Our ultimate hope is to be with Him fully in heaven.

One day we will stand before God face-to-face and enter into His eternal glory. Pain, waiting, and suffering will be no more. Yet the pain, waiting, and suffering we experience here on earth have an eternal purpose: to prepare us and purify us for that day, to mold us more into His image. Understanding this gives us a lens to view everything we walk through in this life: All of it is a tool in the hand of God to be used for our transformation.

1. **In your own words, what do you think is the goal of the Christian life? (Goal = the object of a person's ambition or effort; the aim or desired result.)**

As we talked about in chapter 21 of *So Much Better*, knowing the goal of our lives as Christ-followers is crucial, because it informs the way we see everything. If we believe the goal of our lives is comfort, then we'll be unhappy when things are hard. If we believe the goal of our lives is riches, then we'll be upset when we don't have them. If we believe the goal of our lives is to be liked, then we'll feel unimportant when we aren't. If we believe the goal of our lives is to have all our desires and longings fulfilled, then we'll feel continually unsatisfied in the waiting.

I'll be honest: Though I know none of these is the true goal of the Christian life, at different times, I've lived as if I believe they are. I search for ways to avoid inconveniences, with comfort as my goal. I work hard in hopes that I can get ahead, with financial freedom as my goal. I strive to win people over and let it bother me too much when I'm not someone's cup of tea, with human approval as my goal. I fixate on what I want, with my own desires as my goal.

2. What do you tend to view as the goal of your life, even if you know better? Maybe it's comfort, financial freedom, a certain career achievement, being a wife or a mom, or being liked. A good way to identify the answer to this is to consider what you think about most or what you get frustrated about or down about when you don't have it.

3. Read this verse slowly:

Those whom he foreknew he also predestined to be conformed to the image of his Son, in order that he might be the firstborn among many brothers. And those whom he predestined he also called, and those whom he called he also justified, and those whom he justified he also glorified.

ROMANS 8:29-30

According to this verse, what is God's will for those of us who are in Christ Jesus?

4. Look up the definition of the word *glorify* in a dictionary and write it down.

5. How do we glorify God with our lives? Read John 15:8 and write down your answer.

In Jesus' time, a disciple was a follower or student—someone who not only learned from the teacher's lessons but also modeled their life after the way the teacher lived. It would be like listening to a sermon, then watching a live day-in-the-life vlog of the pastor who preached it. Through the sermon, the pastor teaches truths about Jesus. Through the day-in-the-life vlog, the pastor shows how those truths influence the way he lives.

According to Jesus, we glorify God when our lives and our character are transformed by Him and display His goodness to the world around us. What is the goal of the Christian life? To become like Jesus, to grow into His image. Knowing this gives us the proper perspective when we go through discomfort, misfortune, persecution, or seasons of waiting. God cares about the things we're waiting for, but even more, He cares about who we are becoming while we wait.

6. **How do you see God refining your character through this season of waiting?**

Sometimes we're so set on what we want God to do in our lives that we miss what He is doing. In chapter 17 of *So Much Better*, we look at a story from Luke 5 that shows how God sometimes moves in a way we wouldn't expect, when we wouldn't expect. Let's unpack that story a bit more.

God cares about the things we're waiting for, but even more, He cares about who we are becoming while we wait.

7. **Read Luke 5:1-11 slowly. What do you imagine Peter was feeling when Jesus first came to him? Write down your reflections, along with any observations from the passage that stand out to you.**

Let's revisit a cool piece of contextual information about this passage that adds some insight to the story. I'm not a fisherwoman, and you might not be either, but here's what would be common knowledge to us if we were: Typically, fish hang out in the shallow waters at night. During the daylight hours, they migrate to waters too deep to be caught easily with nets. This is precisely why fishermen such as Simon Peter and his friends fished at night. Conventional wisdom told them to, because this is when they had the highest likelihood of actually catching fish.

When Jesus came to Peter, Peter had already been fishing all night, when it made sense to do so—when he was most likely to bring in a big load. He had worked and waited, and when morning came, he was weary. He was likely feeling defeated too, seeing as his nets were still empty—he had caught nothing. He had given it his best shot when his chances were highest, but now his window had closed. The fish were no longer in the shallows, so Peter would have to wait to try again the next day. Or so he thought.

8. Do you feel a sense of expectancy that God could move in your life right now—either in the way you hope He will or in some other, unexpected way? Or do you feel hopeless, like the window has closed and there's no way God could move in a significant way during this season? Spend some time processing your feelings with the Lord.

Precisely in the moment when Peter counted out the possibility that something new could happen, Jesus came to him and told him to cast his nets. Now remember, Jesus was a carpenter. His area of expertise was construction, not fish. Peter was the fish guy—wouldn't he know best? If Peter, the professional, tried to catch fish all night to no avail, why would the carpenter have any luck now?

9. What has God asked you to do (either in the past or recently) that you've been reluctant to do because it doesn't make sense to you?

The request didn't make sense to Peter, but his obedience in doing so anyway yielded blessing—so much that his once empty boat began to sink because his nets were so full of fish. Peter obeyed not because the circumstances made sense to him but because he believed in the One who gave the instruction. When God directs our efforts, it makes all the difference in the world and produces results we could never manufacture on our own.

10. When God asks you to do something, what typically makes you hesitate in obeying?

11. Read these verses slowly:

> When Simon Peter saw it, he fell down at Jesus' knees, saying, "Depart from me, for I am a sinful man, O Lord." . . . And when they had brought their boats to land, they left everything and followed him.
> **LUKE 5:8, 11**

12. What did the miracle in Peter's life lead him to do?

13. The miracle Jesus performed in Peter's life led Peter to repent and follow Jesus. What do you sense God asking you to turn from as you seek to follow Him more closely?

In chapter 17 of *So Much Better*, we talk about how before Jesus came, people were expecting a Messiah who would overthrow the Roman government. Instead, they got a baby who grew up to become a rabbi, who ultimately gave up His life. Jesus was the leader they longed for, but instead of ruling with an iron scepter, He was a servant leader who humbly laid Himself down.

Sometimes we have such a clear idea of how something will happen that we risk missing it when it actually does. Jesus was different from what many of the Jews were expecting—to the point that some of them missed the very One they had been praying for and waiting for.

Could it be that sometimes our expectations prevent us from seeing what's right in front of us? Could it be that we are prone to miss the good gifts God is graciously trying to give us because they're different from how we expect them to look or how we think they will come about?

14. Do you have a specific idea in mind for how you hope God will answer your prayer? Write it down with as much detail as possible. Spend some time praying through these expectations and ask God how He might want you to hold them with an open hand.

15. Is God presenting possibilities or opportunities in your life that are different from what you had in mind? Write them down and ask God if He might want you to take steps forward in any of these areas.

16. Write down five good things you see God doing in your life right now, even if they aren't the things you're hoping for.

1. ______________________________

2. ______________________________

3. ______________________________

4. ______________________________

5. ______________________________

Let's end this session by meditating on this verse:

> We all, with unveiled face, beholding the glory of the Lord, are being transformed into the same image from one degree of glory to another. For this comes from the Lord who is the Spirit.
> **2 CORINTHIANS 3:18**

Prayer

Lord, help me to remember that the true goal of my life isn't comfort, riches, being liked, or having all my desires satisfied. Help me to remember that the true goal of life is You—being transformed into Your likeness. Help me to see how You are using the circumstances in my life, even the parts I wish You would change, to accomplish this purpose. Show me any areas where I haven't been able to see Your hand because my eyes are so fixed on the one way I hope You will move. Show me where I need to surrender my expectations to embrace the work You want to do. In both my times of waiting and my seasons of fulfillment, help me to behold Your character and continually grow to look more like You. In Jesus' name, amen.

Hide God's Word in Your Heart

Which key verse from this week's study stood out to you most? Highlight it and practice memorizing it this week.

> Those whom he foreknew he also predestined to be conformed to the image of his Son, in order that he might be the firstborn among many brothers. And those whom he predestined he also called, and those whom he called he also justified, and those whom he justified he also glorified.
> **ROMANS 8:29-30**

> By this my Father is glorified, that you bear much fruit and so prove to be my disciples.
> **JOHN 15:8**

> We all, with unveiled face, beholding the glory of the Lord, are being transformed into the same image from one degree of glory to another. For this comes from the Lord who is the Spirit.
> **2 CORINTHIANS 3:18**

Spend some time reflecting on what you learned in this study and what small step you can take toward applying it to your life this week.

WEEK 1

small group lesson plan

Healing in the Waiting

1. Start by having everyone share highs and lows from the week.
2. Invite a volunteer to open in prayer.
3. Watch the video session together.
4. Invite people to share what stood out to them from the video.
5. Have someone read 1 John 1:5-10 out loud, then ask people to share what stands out to them from the passage.

    This is the message we have heard from him and proclaim to you, that God is light, and in him is no darkness at all. If we say we have fellowship with him while we walk in darkness, we lie and do not practice the truth. But if we walk in the light, as he is in the light, we have fellowship with one another, and the blood of Jesus his Son cleanses us from all sin. If we say we have no sin, we deceive ourselves, and the truth is not in us. If we confess our sins, he is faithful and just to forgive us our sins and to cleanse us from all unrighteousness. If we say we have not sinned, we make him a liar, and his word is not in us.

6. Discuss the following questions:
   - What is something you are currently waiting on God for?
   - What has God revealed to you in your waiting? In what areas has He shown you that you're in need of healing?
   - Is confession something you've practiced before? Why or why not? What are your feelings surrounding it?
7. Invite the group to share any prayer requests, then spend some time lifting them up together.

WEEK 2

small group lesson plan

Intimacy in the Waiting

1. Start by having everyone share highs and lows from the week.
2. Invite a volunteer to open in prayer.
3. Watch the video session together.
4. Invite people to share what stood out to them from the video and/or the week's homework.
5. Have someone read John 10:1-11 out loud, then ask people to share what stands out to them from the passage.

"Truly, truly, I say to you, he who does not enter the sheepfold by the door but climbs in by another way, that man is a thief and a robber. But he who enters by the door is the shepherd of the sheep. To him the gatekeeper opens. The sheep hear his voice, and he calls his own sheep by name and leads them out. When he has brought out all his own, he goes before them, and the sheep follow him, for they know his voice. A stranger they will not follow, but they will flee from him, for they do not know the voice of strangers." This figure of speech Jesus used with them, but they did not understand what he was saying to them.

So Jesus again said to them, "Truly, truly, I say to you, I am the door of the sheep. All who came before me are thieves and robbers, but the sheep did not listen to them. I am the door. If anyone enters by me, he will be saved and will go in and out and find pasture. The thief comes only to steal and kill and destroy. I came that they may have life and have it abundantly. I am the good shepherd. The good shepherd lays down his life for the sheep."

6. Discuss the following questions:
   - When in your life have you felt closest to God?
   - Which promise from Ezekiel 34 means the most to you in this season?
   - Do you feel like it's hard for you to hear God's voice? Under what circumstances is it most difficult? Under what circumstances is it easier to hear Him?
7. Invite the group to share any prayer requests, then spend some time lifting them up together.

WEEK 3

small group lesson plan

Faith in the Waiting

1. Start by having everyone share highs and lows from the week.
2. Invite a volunteer to open in prayer.
3. Watch the video session together.
4. Invite people to share what stood out to them from the video and/or the week's homework.
5. Have someone read Hebrews 11:1-12 out loud, then ask people to share what stands out to them from the passage.

> Faith is the assurance of things hoped for, the conviction of things not seen. For by it the people of old received their commendation. By faith we understand that the universe was created by the word of God, so that what is seen was not made out of things that are visible.
>
> By faith Abel offered to God a more acceptable sacrifice than Cain, through which he was commended as righteous, God commending him by accepting his gifts. And through his faith, though he died, he still speaks. By faith Enoch was taken up so that he should not see death, and he was not found, because God

had taken him. Now before he was taken he was commended as having pleased God. And without faith it is impossible to please him, for whoever would draw near to God must believe that he exists and that he rewards those who seek him. By faith Noah, being warned by God concerning events as yet unseen, in reverent fear constructed an ark for the saving of his household. By this he condemned the world and became an heir of the righteousness that comes by faith.

By faith Abraham obeyed when he was called to go out to a place that he was to receive as an inheritance. And he went out, not knowing where he was going. By faith he went to live in the land of promise, as in a foreign land, living in tents with Isaac and Jacob, heirs with him of the same promise. For he was looking forward to the city that has foundations, whose designer and builder is God. By faith Sarah herself received power to conceive, even when she was past the age, since she considered him faithful who had promised. Therefore from one man, and him as good as dead, were born descendants as many as the stars of heaven and as many as the innumerable grains of sand by the seashore.

6. Discuss the following questions:

   - What good do you see God working in your life while you wait?
   - Which do you find more challenging: the waiting itself or knowing whether you should? Why do you think that part is so hard?
   - Which attribute of God do you find most comforting in this season?

7. Invite the group to share any prayer requests, then spend some time lifting them up together.

WEEK 4

small group lesson plan

Humility in the Waiting

1. Start by having everyone share highs and lows from the week.
2. Invite a volunteer to open in prayer.
3. Watch the video session together.
4. Invite people to share what stood out to them from the video and/or the week's homework.
5. Have someone read 1 Peter 5:6-11 out loud, then ask people to share what stands out to them from the passage.

> Humble yourselves, therefore, under the mighty hand of God so that at the proper time he may exalt you, casting all your anxieties on him, because he cares for you. Be sober-minded; be watchful. Your adversary the devil prowls around like a roaring lion, seeking someone to devour. Resist him, firm in your faith, knowing that the same kinds of suffering are being experienced by your brotherhood throughout the world. And after you have suffered a little while, the God of all grace, who has called you to his eternal glory in Christ,

will himself restore, confirm, strengthen, and establish you. To him be the dominion forever and ever. Amen.

6. Discuss the following questions:
    - Do you believe that if you do good, you deserve good, and if you do bad, you deserve bad? Why or why not?
    - How have you seen God humbling you through your waiting?
    - How is your faith being strengthened in this season?
7. Invite the group to share any prayer requests, then spend some time lifting them up together.

WEEK 5

small group lesson plan

Fruitfulness in the Waiting

1. Start by having everyone share highs and lows from the week.
2. Invite a volunteer to open in prayer.
3. Watch the video session together.
4. Invite people to share what stood out to them from the video and/or the week's homework.
5. Have someone read John 15:1-11 out loud, then ask people to share what stands out to them from the passage.

   I am the true vine, and my Father is the vinedresser. Every branch in me that does not bear fruit he takes away, and every branch that does bear fruit he prunes, that it may bear more fruit. Already you are clean because of the word that I have spoken to you. Abide in me, and I in you. As the branch cannot bear fruit by itself, unless it abides in the vine, neither can you, unless you abide in me. I am the vine; you are the branches. Whoever abides in me and I in him, he it is that bears much fruit, for apart from me you can do nothing. If anyone does not abide in me, he is thrown away like a branch and withers; and the branches are gathered, thrown into the fire, and burned. If you abide in me, and my words abide in you, ask whatever you wish, and it will be done for you. By this my Father is glorified, that you bear much fruit and so prove to be my disciples. As the Father has loved me, so have I loved you. Abide in my love. If you keep my commandments, you will abide in my love, just as I have kept my Father's commandments and abide in his love. These things I have spoken to you, that my joy may be in you, and that your joy may be full.

6. Discuss the following questions:
   - Why do you think it often feels like pruning is punishment?
   - What is God currently pruning from your life?
   - Through what practices do you feel most connected to Jesus?
7. Invite the group to share any prayer requests, then spend some time lifting them up together.

WEEK 6

small group lesson plan

Transformation in the Waiting

1. Start by having everyone share highs and lows from the week.
2. Invite a volunteer to open in prayer.
3. Watch the video session together.
4. Invite people to share what stood out to them from the video and/or the week's homework.
5. Have someone read Romans 8:26-30 out loud, then ask people to share what stands out to them from the passage.

   The Spirit helps us in our weakness. For we do not know what to pray for as we ought, but the Spirit himself intercedes for us with groanings too deep for words. And he who searches hearts knows what is the mind of the Spirit, because the Spirit intercedes for the saints according to the will of God. And we know that for those who love God all things work together for good, for those who are called according to his purpose. For those whom he foreknew he also predestined to be conformed to the image of his Son, in order that he might be the firstborn among many brothers. And those whom he predestined he also called, and those whom he called he also justified, and those whom he justified he also glorified.

6. Discuss the following questions:
   - What tends to be the goal of your life?
   - How do you see God transforming your character through an (as of yet) unanswered prayer?
   - Share a way you see God working in your life that's different from what you expected.
7. Invite the group to share any prayer requests, then spend some time lifting them up together.

about the author

Kaci Nicole Harlow is a follower of Jesus, wife, mama, Christian YouTuber, writer, and speaker whose greatest joy is seeing lives transformed through knowing Jesus Christ. What began as a small step of obedience in 2015—creating a simple online blog called *Kaci Nicole*—has since grown into a global ministry dedicated to helping people know Jesus more deeply, grow in His likeness, and make Him known.

When Kaci first started writing, her heart was simply to encourage others by sharing what she was learning in her own walk with God and in His Word. Today, her ministry includes in-depth Bible studies, topical studies, and Christian living videos—all rooted in Scripture and created with a desire to point people back to Christ. On her popular *Bible Study with Me* series on YouTube, Kaci has walked through several books of the Bible verse by verse, inviting viewers to study alongside her and discover the richness of God's Word for themselves.

A thoughtful communicator, Kaci has also spoken at women's events, churches, and conferences, where she shares biblical truth with warmth, depth, and relatable honesty. Her passion is to help others see that Jesus isn't just part of life—He is life. She encourages her audience—primarily young women—to seek Him in every season: in singleness and marriage, career and motherhood, joy and sorrow, big decisions and everyday rhythms. Kaci believes that a life with Jesus is of surpassing worth—the only true source of peace, joy, and identity. Through every video, written piece, and speaking opportunity, Kaci's hope is to help people know God more through His Word and grow in His likeness.

Kaci and her husband, Tyler, along with their two children, Judah and Savannah, live in San Diego, where they are deeply involved in their local church. They love serving, hosting, and doing ministry together—their heart is to live out the gospel in community and to help others do the same. Their favorite ministry is family—living out God's design for marriage, building a life together for God's glory, and raising their children in the Lord. Kaci loves matcha, puns, eggs, traveling, all things home, and good heart-to-hearts.

Connect with Kaci:
kacinicole.com
YouTube: @kacinicole
Instagram: @kacinicole

journaling pages